AHEAD

How to Make the Most of Your College Experience 2013

Learning is a lifelong necessity.

Ernie Marino

Enjoy the journey + all the best Jay + Sally Douglass

Dr. Ernest M. Marino

Printed in the United States of America
First Edition: March 2013

ISBN: 978-0-9897675-0-7

Dedication

To Lyn, without whose help, love,
and support this book
would never have been finished.

Preface

A message to parents and students:

We live in difficult and interesting times. Since there is intense global competition for admission to post-graduate programs and, subsequently, suitable employment, students must be diligent and focused in their studies. They really have no other choice.

Despite the best efforts of many dedicated teachers and administrators, we have a failed K-12 government monopoly of our educational system. We are seriously behind internationally in science, math, and reading. We are a nation at risk in many ways.

I wrote this book not only for conscientious students who want to attend professional schools (medical, dental, law, nursing, chiropractic, osteopathic, etc.) and STEM (science, technology, engineering, and math) graduate programs, but also for those conscientious students interested in doing their best in any field of study.

Contents

My Story 9

Philosophy 12

Vision.. 13

Objectives 15

Understanding.. 17

Electronic Disfigurement of the Mind.................................18

Excellify 21

Improve Your Vocabulary 23

Study Aids 25

Computer Literacy 27

Reading 28

Writing 31

Who Am I, Why Am I Here, Where Am I Going............................33

Stay Away From Jerks 34

Basic Life Skills 35

Enrichment..37

Economics 40

Getting Better Grades 45

Starting Your Own Shorthand System –Some Suggestions 49

Taking Exams...53

Selecting A Profession or A Livelihood...............................55

Lifelong Learning 57

Graciousness 59

Principles of Success 61

Heroes 63

Investing 65

Gratitude 67

ADD/ADHD 69

Conclusion 71

Suggested Reading 73

About The Author 75

My Story

I completed my high school education in 1957 in the New York City public school system and was adequately prepared for college except, in retrospect, in comprehensive reading skills. My college board scores were above average. My high school grades were very good. I was the first person in my family and among 20 cousins to go to college. I was the oldest of three brothers. One brother dropped out of college during his first semester, and my younger brother – the brightest one of us — died after his freshman year. To earn money during high school, I mowed lawns, did yard work, sold ice cream, cleaned stables, and "puddled" cement for highway construction. It didn't take me long to realize that a college education was crucial for earning a good living. My grandparents had promised my father that he could go to Yale, but the Great Depression dashed those dreams, and, consequently, he did not even finish high school. He was quietly bitter about this right up until he died at the age of 90. As I was growing up, he always used the words "when you go to college," and that comment became a part of me.

I was accepted at Yale University, Dartmouth University, and Wesleyan University in Middletown, Connecticut. It never would have occurred to me to apply to Wesleyan had it not been for a chance encounter with a friend who was going there. After I visited Wesleyan, I decided that's where I wanted to go. It was a small school, and I liked its atmosphere and camaraderie. At the time, Wesleyan was an all-male school, which probably was a good thing for me. Looking back, I realize I did not have the maturity to attend a coed school.

At Wesleyan, we had to work hard for our grades. There were no easy courses. It was during my first two years that I formulated some study techniques that enabled my being accepted into the University of Pennsylvania dental school, and later into a graduate dental program at Boston University, specializing in periodontics. Between dental school and graduate school, I studied oral pathology for a year with the American Cancer Society.

I was grateful for my Wesleyan education and appreciated the many dedicated professors who taught my classes, many of whom were department heads. I never looked back on my Wesleyan years. I wasn't sure why until I attended my 50th college reunion. It was recounted that Victor Butterfield, my college president, commented that if our four years at Wesleyan were the best years of our lives, then Wesleyan failed us miserably. I had to mature, take responsibility, and become disciplined. Now I can see that getting through those difficult years prepared me for the rigors of an additional seven years of study.

I was a trustee for a decade at Applewild School in Fitchburg, MA. Many teachers there took a salary cut in order to work there because they knew they were appreciated and had autonomy in their classrooms. The trustees were mostly parents with direct input into day-to-day operations. Talented businessmen guided the finances exceptionally well. Teachers were listened to and respected. Poor behavior by students was not tolerated and some students were dismissed. Classes went to the ninth grade, and most students were able to go to the secondary school of their choice, many of which were prestigious.

I had originally moved my family to a small New England town because its public school was reputed to be excellent.

In the first and second grades, my daughter would come home from school each day with only drawings as evidence of having been in class. She was taught very little with regard to reading, writing, and math. We felt this was unacceptable, so we sent her, and later her younger brother and sister, to Applewild School and subsequently to Phillips Andover Academy. The education they received at these schools contributed to their acceptance into the Massachusetts Institute of Technology and to the University of California at Berkeley.

Most of the techniques I outline in the following pages are straightforward. Learn how to learn, and you will have more options in life and more opportunities for success.

Philosophy

I did not have a clearly defined philosophy of living when I was in college. Through mistakes, pain, trial and error, observing and thinking, my philosophy evolved. Over time, I came to clearly realize that I am 100% responsible for all that I think, say, and do. No one else can think for me, speak for me, or act for me. No one can respond for me when I am called. I am my own sovereign. I am the "Master of my Fate and the Captain of my Soul." I am unique and will create my own life using my own vision.

At the start of my Rotary meeting each week, we recite something called the "Four-Way Test": "Of the things we think, say, and do, (1) Is it the truth? (2) Is it fair to all concerned? (3) Will it build good will and better friendships? (4) Will it be beneficial to all concerned?" In your dealings with others, you will meet these four types of people: (1) competent and ethical (2) incompetent and ethical (3) competent and unethical (4) incompetent and unethical. Be very, very discerning.

My philosophy of living is rooted in Judeo-Christian values, our Consititution, and Free Market Capitalism. Keep refining your philosophy of thinking, living, and judging. Your philosophy will evolve over a period of time. Make sure your philosophy is consistent with your fundamental values. You will sleep better, be more at peace with yourself, and be more successful when your vision becomes a reality.

Vision

A personal vision of what you want from life is the first step to success. You will encounter numerous choices you will have to sift through carefully in order to clarify your vision. In my case, it was clear to me that I wanted to work for myself and be a professional. It was in my senior year of college that I chose dentistry, after first considering medicine.

Your vision should be written and reviewed daily. It should bring tears to your eyes. It should be written in the present tense, as if it is already happening. 'For example, "I am in medical school in September of 2017. The decisions I made to go to class and study diligently have paid off. The difficult classes I took put me in a better position to be accepted into medical school."

Many studies have clearly demonstrated that having a written vision for the future puts you on a more solid path to success in life. If you are not sure what you want to do early on in college, simply write a general vision that you can modify later. For example, "My interest in science put me in a position to work in a field demanding scientific understanding. With so many possibilities ahead of me, my diligence has put me in a position to have many job offers. By focusing on science, I have several excellent offers from major firms. My diligence and planning have definitely paid off."

Make your vision detailed and emotional. It can be either a few paragraphs or several pages. And you must own it! Give careful thought to your vision and remember that it isn't cast in concrete. It is always in a state of "becoming." Stay focused on learning using your vision as a filter. A user-friendly blueprint for writing your vision can be found in the section entitled "The Fundamentals of Success" in Jack Canfield's book, Success Principles. You are the only one who can determine what defines success in your mind and in your life.

Objectives

Your objectives in going to college are straightforward:

- Go with a serious sense of purpose. You are in college to acquire a solid grounding in subject matter that will enable you to get into the graduate or professional school of your choice or to get a good job when you graduate.
- Learn how to learn. Whatever you do, you will always need to learn more in your field. There will always be advances in your chosen discipline that will require you to learn more. Learn how to study efficiently and effectively.
- Balance science-oriented courses with the arts and humanities. The arts will enrich your life, open your heart, and expand your sensibilities.
- Develop your human relations skills. Since you will always have to deal with people, start acquiring the skills that will genuinely help you get along with others.
- Start to position yourself for success. Understand the principles for success.
- Ultimately, you want to be self-reliant, at peace with yourself and the world around you, and be able to think for yourself. Do not fall into the "entitlement trap." This losing mentality will hamper your quest for success.

College can be a wonderful place in which to grow intellectually and prepare for life. High grades, of course, are a necessary part of this package.

Understanding

"With all thy getting, get understanding."(Proverbs 4:7) This biblical quote appears at the top of the editorial page of _Forbes_ magazine and clearly guides Steve Forbes in his successful life. I have read this publication from cover to cover for several decades; I urge you to do the same.

Understanding is not simply accumulating facts, but rather fitting the facts into your reality. This can be a lifelong process. There is a mind-boggling amount of information out there, including much disinformation and misinformation. It is important to have reliable sources of information and opinions to guide you.

Electronic Disfigurement of the Mind

The benefits of the digital age are exceptional, but there is a down-side. Electronic Disfigurement of the Mind (EDM) is how I describe the net effect of distorted negative media in all forms – print, television, radio, videos, the internet, speech, and various combinations thereof.

The concept of EDM is not a new one. I formulated it over thirty years ago. My son at age seven was watching too much television. I pleaded with him to limit his viewing time, but that did not work. I did not exercise my parental authority – I was not a Tiger Dad. What I noticed were the ridiculous sounds and odd mannerisms he exhibited. They actually frightened me. Finally after many years of no progress, I came up with a plan: I bribed him. I told him I would give him a thousand dollars if he stopped watching television. He could use the money for his college fund or for clothing, but not for junk toys. He abided by the agreement. Since he was bored, he started reading and won the book prize in his eighth grade class for having read over sixty books.

Children are clever. Instead of watching TV, my children occasionally watched rented movies. Too many of these videos were violent and grisly. It was not what they sought, but what prevailed in the marketplace.

There are many areas of deliberate mental disfigurement:

- Political correctness – a clear attempt to sacrifice free speech on the altar of non-discerning, vapid politeness. This is an emotional crippler. Many people are overly sensitive and easily offended – often a no-win situation.
- Constant challenge of cherished cultural and religious beliefs.
- Indoctrination, brainwashing, propagandizing, and the deliberate dumbing-down of our young people at all levels of education. This thesis was brilliantly developed by Thomas Sowell in Inside American Education. Students are taught to be all-inclusive of everything with little discernment of what is right or what is wrong. Too often, they become morally adrift.
- Constant din of cacophonous sound. Very few media sounds are soothing. There is no substitute for the quiet of nature. The collective sounds of the media are not relaxing. The repetitive theme songs that are the hallmark of various sports channels and programs, for example, are thumping and discordant.

- Content manipulation. This is seen mainly on TV news shows with deliberate bias and selective reporting. If you are given information that is deliberately false and misleading, yet you believe it to be true, it becomes impossible to understand what is going on around you. In conversation, you can get an idea of where people are coming from by simply asking them what their news sources are.
- Economic distortions. Most people are clueless about economics. Too many people think the wealthy are the cause of their financial woes. They do not understand that a government cannot spend more than it brings in without having future problems, just as individuals cannot spend more than they earn for very long without going bankrupt. Countries fall apart after overspending for a few decades. We are in the midst of enormous economic disarray.
- Hyperconnectivity. People like to stay in touch, but hundreds of text messages, tweets, Facebook postings, emails, etc., have to be limited. These excesses are leading to a fragmentation of thought.
- Being "deviced," that is, being addicted to the use of a computer, tablet, MP3 player, or phone. This results in wasting time, getting sidetracked, and withdrawing from reality.

The simplest solution to ridding oneself of these disfigurements is to minimize exposure to the various media and computer nonsense. Parents will be doing their children a great service. It will be difficult, to be sure, but definitely worth the effort.

Despite the disfigurements, there is a tremendous up-side: an elevation of consciousness and the growth of knowledge. People are more connected and more aware of their humanity. They are developing a universal consciousness and an awareness of what constitutes positivism and integrity in life situations.

Excellify

In everything I think, say, or do, I try to make improvements. It is not a preoccupation or an effort, but a state of mindfulness. I try to be "in the moment" as much as possible. I have made a lot of improvement since I stopped paying too much attention to the negativities of news broadcasts.

There is very little that cannot be improved upon. The tone of your voice in all of the little interactions that occur every day is one example. Whenever I am in a drive-through lane at a coffee shop, a check-out counter at the supermarket, or get a phone call from a telemarketer, I try to be pleasant and cheerful. At the supermarket, I always smile at the cashier, say hello, and ask, "How are you holding up today?" When I visit my elderly friend, I always ask him at some point in our conversation, "Are you behaving today?" No matter what he says, I jokingly tell him I don't believe him. We chat about little things, and I always try to get him to smile or laugh – and I usually succeed.

When I perform mundane tasks, I'm always asking myself, "How can I improve this?" When I make our daily breakfast, I set the table with care, prepare a little fruit plate, and cook the eggs as best I can. I do not allow my chores to become drudgery or a nuisance. Recently, in thawing frozen pipes on three separate occasions, I did not lose my temper or use foul language (but I thought about it). I approached each thawing with a positive mindset and figured out little shortcuts to make the job easier.

During my professional career, I made countless improvements in my surgical procedures. There were so many subtle improvements over time that most patients recovered uneventfully and without fanfare. Patients who were on the verge of losing their teeth over thirty years ago still have their teeth today. I took pride in my surgical skills, but I was also thankful that I had the gift of dexterity. Even so, I always felt that no matter how good my surgical outcomes were, there was always room for improvement.

The attitude of seeking constant improvement I refer to as "excellification." I try to practice this concept in everything I do. Life is more interesting and much more enjoyable when you "excellify." I want my word to become part of our language. Instead of playing a game "to win," play it "to excel"! Make "excellification" part of your mindset, too.

Improve Your Vocabulary

Successful people have extensive vocabularies. A working knowledge of words will enrich your understanding of the world around you. Growing up, I had an interest in using more descriptive words, but I just learned them randomly. It was very inefficient.

My vocabulary breakthrough came during my senior year in high school. In the local bookstore, I discovered Thirty Days to a More Powerful Vocabulary, by Norman Lewis and Wilfred Funk. This small paperback book opened my mind to the richness of words and expanded my limited intellectual awareness. It profoundly changed my understanding of the world around me. Written over 50 years ago, Thirty Days to a More Powerful Vocabulary is still a classic and should be included in every high school curriculum. In this volume, words are logically grouped into categories, and practice exercises reinforce the learning. Without complaining, each of my children completed Thirty Days to a More Powerful Vocabulary by the time they were in eighth grade.

Another book I used was Word Power Made Easy, by Norman Lewis. Originally published in 1949, the first edition was cumbersome to use, but the revised expanded version is a gem. Word Power Made Easy gives the etymological background of words, which helps with word associations, and the book's structure makes it very user-friendly.

No matter where you are in your life or schooling, I would recommend Thirty Days to a More Powerful Vocabulary and Word Power Made Easy as being essential for intellectual development.

Study Aids

It is important as you study to have resources to assist you when you do not understand the subject matter. If you have done your assignments, taken good notes, and reviewed them often, you should need only a few resources.

- The most important resource is you. Put in a little more time and effort into comprehending the subject matter. As much as possible, get used to solving problems on your own.
- A classmate or "study buddy" should be your next resource.

- Upperclassmen who have taken the course you're having difficulty with can give you pointers, especially if you have the same professor.
- The teaching assistant, if there is one, can guide you to clearer understanding of the problem.
- The professor who is giving the course is the ultimate resource. Do not hesitate to make an appointment should you need clarification or help.
- Use the videos available from the Khan Academy, found online (www.khanacademy.org).
- Seek counsel when necessary, but always think for yourself.
- Learning is not always direct. Make adjustments as you go along.

In addition to the above resources, you may want to do additional reading in the library. The internet should be used as a primary source of knowledge infrequently at best. Wikipedia, the most widely used online resource, is not always reliable, since anyone can make or modify entries or existing text. Published hard copies — books, papers, monographs, etc. — should be your primary resources overall. The internet lacks the ability, by itself, to convey the depth of many topics.

If you develop a network of classmates, upperclassmen, and instructors to help you, you will be able to sort out any difficulties with subject matter. If you develop a curiosity with regard to the subject matter and use the library, the internet (sparingly), and learn to think for yourself, you have a recipe for success.

Computer Literacy

As simplistic as this might sound, using a computer efficiently is critical to your success. A computer is not just for surfing the internet or for social networking. Much of what you are required to do in school will involve word processing. Proper finger placement on the keyboard will double and triple your output. Take a formal keyboarding class or find an application that teaches this critical skill.

You should also learn how to store and retrieve documents. Scanning class notes into your laptop or PC may be helpful. You can then categorize them by subject, theme, or any other criterion. (Your handwritten notes, however, are still your best bet for studying.)

Reading

Reading was my biggest obstacle in college, even though I learned to read before I went to elementary school. In the first grade, we were taught to read one word at a time, rather than group words into phrases or thoughts. Unfortunately, this practice stayed with me, and I read very slowly. Since there were very few books in our house when I was growing up, I was not encouraged to improve my skills.

Despite my reading deficiencies, as a child I was curious and read excerpts in encyclopedias about different topics. I read about gunpowder and knew that sulphur, potassium nitrate, and charcoal were necessary ingredients. I went to the local pharmacy at age seven and bought these items. Enlisting my cousin as my cohort, I actually made gunpowder. We played with it in our garage and almost started a fire. The fire department came, and I hid in my parents' bedroom, assuming they were coming to take me away. Of course, no lesson was learned: After outgrowing gunpowder, my cousin and I decided to look into TNT. Luckily, we weren't able to find all the ingredients, because we probably would have blown ourselves up in the process.

I did not finish many of my college literature reading assignments. To compensate for my poor reading skills, I would skim over an assignment, gleaning highlights of what I thought was important. When I had longer reading assignments, I would pre-read. I would read the first few paragraphs of a chapter and then the last few paragraphs. I would read topic sentences and concluding sentences of the paragraphs in between. At least I was able to get a good overview of a particular chapter or passage.

I was able to complete reading assignments in science, art, philosophy, logic, and economics because they were shorter ones. I enjoyed learning, but the deficiency in my reading skills was a hindrance to my intellectual growth. Even though I was a good student in high school, ranking highly in a class of several hundred students, my overall deficiency in reading slowed my learning.

I took an Evelyn Wood Speed Reading Course after I graduated from dental school, and it worked. I dramatically increased my reading speed, but I didn't continue to practice these new skills. Consequently, I reverted back to my slow reading habits. Still seeking to improve my skills, several years ago I purchased a reading program called "Eye-Q," which was advertised to improve reading comprehension and SAT scores. It was well-designed and worthwhile. More and more of these programs are available, both online and as apps for smartphones and tablets. You should research them if any part of my story sounds familiar to you. I'm thankful that my persistence in improvement paid off – over the last 40 years, I have accumulated several thousand books on a myriad of subjects. I can sincerely call myself an avid reader now.

Many schools have remedial reading programs that may be of help if you need it. See what programs are available at your college. If you need assistance, talk to your counselors or advisers to see if any of these programs might be a fit for you.

Writing

Writing was always difficult for me, that is, until recently. I do not consider myself adept at writing, but I am making some progress since I started working with a "Getting Things Done" coach.

When I was in college, I would spend weeks writing a term paper for an English class or a Humanities class and get only a B or B- grade. On the other hand, one of my schoolmates, Robin Cook (yes, THE Robin Cook!) would, for example, tell me on a Saturday when we were coming home from a football game that he had a term paper due on Monday. After spending only two or three hours writing the paper (sometimes on the team bus), Robin would get an A or A+. Clearly, his writing skills developed earlier than mine.

When I was a practicing periodontist, I wrote over 30,000 reports regarding my patients. These did not require creativity as much as they did thoroughness, accurate reporting of findings, diagnoses, and suitable treatment plans. I dictated my reports immediately, while the patient was still in the chair. Dictating on the spot was efficient, not just because it saved time, but because my findings were fresh in my mind. There was no need to struggle at the end of the day with a pile of charts and try to remember the minute details of each case. This was appreciated by both patients and referring dentists alike.

Here are some suggestions to help your writing:

- Enter all your thoughts, facts, and ideas that pertain to your writing assignment into your computer. Rearrange the information into a logical outline. Let it sit for a day or two, look at it again, make edits and modifications, and start writing from it.
- Write thoughts, facts, and ideas on 3x5 cards. When you have gathered enough information, arrange them in a logical order as your outline.
- Take a blank sheet of paper and start writing down all your thoughts, facts, and ideas as they come to you. Rearrange the information into a logical outline. You can "cut and paste" sentences and paragraphs with scissors and glue.
- When you write your paper, make sure you understand the use of topic sentences that convey the essence of the larger paragraph.
- Write as if you are speaking to someone and you want that person to listen to what you are saying.
- Reports for science/lab courses are somewhat easier. Before going into any lab class, read the assignment over, so you won't be wasting time during the lab itself. Experimental designs vary, but they all have the need for careful observation and recording of empirical data. You will learn how your data supports or doesn't support your hypothesis (scientific method). Junk science is rampant, and a good background in what constitutes the scientific method will give you an edge.

Your ability to communicate effectively, persuasively, and efficiently is crucial in this information age we live in. Writing skills – including word processing and keyboard skills — take time to develop.

Who Am I,
Why Am I Here,
Where Am I Going

These perennial questions have occupied man's mind forever. We seek to understand the mysteries of life and make sense of our own lives and of the world around us. The answers are out there, and it takes time to sort everything out. Some people have a simplicity of faith, love, and charity, and instinctively understand these mysteries. They are saintly role models for the rest of us. To be sure, these questions are difficult to fathom when there are so many problems in our lives.

Your insights into these questions will unfold in time. Our responses affect our happiness. Cravings and aversions are big factors in how we respond. When we respond negatively to the vicissitudes of day-to-day living, things become more difficult. When we deal constructively with setbacks that we all have, outcomes are less traumatic. If you can manage your life positively and be a good role model for others, you are making a genuine contribution. There are many avenues available – seek them out. For the most part, unless you become involved, things will always remain as they are, not as you want them to be. Understanding these matters will help you find inner peace.

Stay Away From Jerks

Too many people do not have a clear sense of purpose. Parties, carousing, and drinking are their predominate behaviors. These jerks are everywhere, and their actions reveal them. I was one of those jerks for a while, but I always had the realization that I had to study and be diligent in order to get ahead in life.

Do not fall into the trap of accepting people who have negative values systems and mindsets. Trying to get along with everyone – being a "people pleaser" – is a losing strategy, and you will have wasted a lot of time accommodating people who could care less about you and the world around them.

Be judgmental. We are told not to judge others. That in itself, if you think about it, is a judgment. Here is what you have to realize: For many, lying is a matter of routine and totally acceptable as a means to an end

Chart your own course in life and stay away from the negative nabobs, because they will never go away on their own, and they will block your path to success.

Basic Life Skills

There are quite a few things you can do that will position you for lifelong success:

- First, you need to know where you are going in your life. You, and only you, can determine that. That will be your vision.
- You must realize that you have to put effort into what you do. If you are indifferent to your work, it will be difficult – if not impossible – to advance.
- Grow your strengths. My strengths in periodontics were my surgical skills and my ability to relate to my patients. We each have unique strengths, talents, and ambitions; develop the ones that work for you.
- Go the "extra mile." Do more than is expected of you.
- Be positive. Life is difficult enough, so do your work with good cheer. You will feel better and get more done in the process.
- Stay away from negative people. They will diminish your ability to get your work done. A problem will always need solving, but a problem is not the source of the negativity: Your attitude is.
- Nourish your spiritual self. Pray, meditate, affirm.

- Take care of your physical self. It is hard to function well when you are not healthy. Take the time to exercise. Eight Minutes in the Morning by Jorge Cruise is an easy and effective exercise program and requires no special equipment or venue. You might want to try yoga, aerobics, an intramural sport, or just walking. The main thing is to get out and move.
- Continue to learn about your chosen discipline. Take continuing education courses or workshops on a regular basis.
- Keep a balance in work, love, play, and spirituality.
- Eat healthy and take high-quality dietary supplements. Eat fresh fruits and vegetables as well as quality meats and fish. Organic is best, but it takes time to sort out what is truly organic, since the terms "organic" and "natural" have been corrupted. Make sure you know your food sources.
- Confront and resolve emotional and other issues you have. If you don't deal with your problems, they can destroy you or at least significantly hold you back. Seek competent professional help if necessary.
- Become involved in your community.
- Keep developing your human relations skills. Never sacrifice your core beliefs merely to get along with someone. It won't work.
- If you work for someone else, work for them as if the business were your own. You will enjoy your work more and you will be more likely to advance. You also will be in a better position to start your own successful business.

Enrichment

I took several courses in college that enriched my life considerably. As a science-oriented student, I was only dimly aware of the arts and the humanities. I did, however, have an interest in art and music.

I enrolled in an art history survey course that concentrated on 18th through 20th century artists. It was well-taught, and I developed an appreciation for the artists who depicted life as they saw it and interpreted it. I marveled at the skills they had. It took a while to adjust to the less precise terminology that artists used. I had initially laughed at the vagueness of their language, but slowly developed an appreciation for how the artists looked at the world and how they and the art historians described their creativity.

With my interest in art piqued, I decided to take a painting course. In class, my efforts led me to appreciate abstract expressionism. The relationships between color, form, and composition were intriguing. My teacher liked what I painted and encouraged me to go to Yale and study during the summer with Josef Albers. I declined because I wanted to be with my friends — a decision that I regretted in later years — not realizing that I could have studied with an acknowledged master. Fifty years after my college graduation, my desire to paint has resurfaced, and I am pursuing painting again in a small way.

Another course that enriched my life forever was a music appreciation course. We worked our way from Gregorian chant to music of the 20th century. The transition from the Classical to the Romantic Era was carefully explained, as were other clearly defined musical periods. The richness of music enlivened me. I have had no formal musical training in my life, but this course opened my ears to the beauty and rapture of master composers' works. During dental school, I would often go the Academy of Music in Philadelphia and experience the genius of Eugene Ormandy and other guest conductors. An usher knew when certain ticket holders would not be attending the concerts, and for five dollars I was usually able to get a seat in the first balcony. There is nothing as thrilling as a live performance. For 20 years I attended the performances of the Manchester (New Hampshire) Choral Society. The brilliant Lisa Wolff directed choral pieces that defy description, at least by me. Recordings of these performances do not do justice to their richness, although they do bring to mind many sublime moments. Since my wife sang in the ensemble, I attended every performance. I have no singing talent, but I trusted my ears and was deeply moved by the music. Our church choir, under the direction of Mark Andrew Cleveland, an accomplished professional singer himself in the Boston area, performs anthems from sacred repertoire each Sunday. These, too, are works of art, and I often find myself having to refrain from applauding in church!

Although not "enrichment," per se, a course in logic was helpful to me in understanding the manipulation of language. In the same way, a philosophy course helped me learn how to think in general.

I would encourage all students to take enrichment courses in the arts and humanities – dance, theater, music, painting, film, writing, etc. Such enrichment courses will add joy and an insight into the world in general for the science-oriented student.

Economics

More nonsense, misinformation, disinformation, propaganda, rhetoric, and brainwashing appear in the economic realm than anywhere else. A course in free market capitalism (Austrian School of Economics) will help you navigate through the economic labyrinth we are in.

If you are able take a course in free market capitalism, by all means do so. Unfortunately, it is unlikely you will find one. Despite this, any course in economics will familiarize you with some of the various terms that you will come across in your reading.

Some of these terms and ideas which will help you understand economics include fiscal policy and monetary policy, Keynesianism vs. free market capitalism, depression, recession, inflation, deflation, prime rate, national debt, asset value, capitalization, stocks and bonds, margin requirements, gold standard, gross domestic product, exchange rates, role of the Federal Reserve, unfunded liabilities, and futures markets.

It is crucial to understand how the private sector funds the public sector. There are two major economic theories: Keynesianism and free market capitalism. Keynesianism operates under the belief that a small group of people (government, etc.) can create wellbeing by taking from the providers (taxpayers – individuals, small businesses, and corporations) and redistributing that wealth to help those who do not have it (social justice, entitlements, etc.). Our national debt is over $16 trillion, and our economic situation is dire — high unemployment, almost 50 million people on food stamps, an increase in bankruptcy filings, to name a few. If spending other people's money worked, we would be living in a utopia. Instead, too many people are mired in misery and looking for honest solutions. Spending money that isn't there and overtaxing wage earners and small businesses are tactics that have failed miserably. These policies of tax-and-spend have increased poverty and fostered dependency. This is Keynesianism in all its splendor, an abysmal failure rife with government waste and inefficiency. This is the public sector destroying the private sector with incessant demands for more money. There are too many people who do nothing and produce nothing who expect others to provide for them. They have an entitlement mentality. In a socialist society, an individual gets paid even when if that individual barely produces anything, and can't be fired from his or her job. Incompetence is the result.

The better economic theory is free market capitalism, in which individuals and groups (small businesses, corporations) are free to buy and sell from each other with minimum public interference. Big Government does not work. According to Ludwig von Mises, government is a "negation of liberty," whereas the free market creates abundance by offering choices and solving problems. The free market works best with sound money, private property rights, the Rule of Law, the ability to make contracts, small government, free trade, school choice, and limited taxation.

The federal misallocation of money in the billions of dollars did not help failing "green" firms like Solyndra, a solar panel manufacturer, which, having produced no solar panels, lost $535 million of government money. So, after having an infusion of $535 million, Solyndra still went bankrupt. Governments can't predict winners and losers; what government mostly does is create losers - increasing poverty and destroying the economic fabric of our wonderful country.

Free market capitalism was championed by Ludwig von Mises, who explained how the free market worked and socialism did not. In his book Human Action, the fundamental thesis is that our economic activities are governed by various price feedbacks. This feedback enables a business owner to make corrections to the business accordingly. Under Keynesian socialism, there is no real price feedback. This was also clearly explained by economist George Gilder in a recent National Review article. Profit and loss and revenue streams need to be understood as feedback. Gilder also notes that lowering taxes, beyond any doubt, always increases revenue. Today, large institutions are considered to be too big to be allowed to fail, yet the individual is too small to be helped by lowering his taxes. High taxes create poverty, which, in turn, pushes people into dependency. Friedrich von Hayek wrote about what he called the "Fatal Conceit" in his book of the same name, stating that small groups of people (government) cannot manage the affairs of larger groups (populace). Central planners cannot take most of your money and redistribute it equitably. Lies are necessary to promote this flawed redistributionist ideology. Thus, the Fatal Conceit has become the Fatal Deceit.

The average person paying taxes has to work more than four months before he can earn money to pay bills or just survive. He is an economic slave. This is the new serfdom as explained by Friedrich von Hayek in his book The Road to Serfdom, and updated by Daniel Hannan in The New Road to Serfdom. A clear overview of free market capitalism is outlined by Steve Forbes in his recent book Freedom Manifesto. He should be our president! Stick with Steve. The editorials in his eponymous magazine are pertinent to today's issues. His idea of a flat tax would revolutionize our economy.

Another must-read is Free To Choose, by Milton and Rose Friedman. In it, the authors state that when people are free to sell or buy a product or a service, the market itself sorts out winners and losers. You cannot coerce equality. Sadly, coercion is becoming the norm today.

Ask your parents or elders if they feel they are better off today than they were twenty or thirty years ago. If they worked in the private sector, it is likely you will get an honest response – "No, we are not better off." Fifty years ago, a thrifty working father and a stay-at-home mother could afford to send their children to college. They could even have a reasonably-priced vacation home. Today, with both parents and the college-bound student working, loans are almost always necessary to finance education.

Our current national debt is over 16 trillion dollars with recent annual deficits of over a trillion dollars. A Bloomberg News report, containing information taken directly from government websites, showed per capita indebtedness of over $125,000.

This is where we are now. The heavy hand of the government is intruding into all aspects of our lives. There are 73,000 pages in the US tax code alone, as well as 200,000 pages of rules and regulations. There is no price/revenue feedback to determine the efficacy of government programs. The government states that it is the intention that counts, not the result. Can you imagine running a business that way?

Once you understand the basics of free market capitalism, you will be in a better position to understand our economy. You will also be in a better position to influence others in their understanding of the issues.

To summarize:

- Generally speaking, it is unlikely that governments can spend money wisely.
- As government grows, the quality of life declines because governments are wasteful and inefficient.

- Government exists only for itself. The government receives money from taxing the private sector and then creates poverty and inefficiency.
- Government seemingly never has enough of your money.
- Inflation is rearing its ugly head and destroying the purchasing power of money.
- The Federal Reserve, a private central bank, has failed America. There are too many people in politics and elsewhere engaged in legalized theft.
- An economic "Black Swan Event" (an unexpected event that is catastrophic) appears inevitable
- America is losing her commanding heights to control her own financial sovereignty.
- We are evolving into a collective in which you pay other people, through taxation, to run your life and dictate how you should live.

Getting Better Grades

This chapter contains the essence of how to get better grades. The two key study habits to cultivate are:

1. Taking very good notes efficiently;
2. Reviewing your notes systematically.

In addition, you must adhere to the basics:

1. Go to class;
2. Get assignments in on time;
3. Study diligently;
4. Minimize wasteful activities (excessive partying, drinking, etc.)

Of all the basics, going to class was the most crucial for me. I found it difficult to use other people's notes. There was no real substitute for going to class and taking comprehensive notes myself.

Reviewing your notes in a timely fashion is one of the most important study habits to develop. In my first year of college, I had trouble adjusting to course work and studying for exams. What changed my education forever was a comment in a book on studying that I found at the college bookstore. It was the simple observation that you'll remember 50% or more of your notes if you review them within 24 hours of writing them down. As a result, I started reviewing my notes as soon as possible after class:

- I underlined key phrases;
- I wrote new words and ideas in the margins or at the end;
- I reviewed the notes from the previous class before the next class, usually while I was waiting for the class to start; and
- I reviewed my notes when I worked on assignments.

By the time an exam came around, I had reviewed my notes 20 or 30 times. Repetition is the mother of learning. Learning the material was easier because I did it incrementally without any pressure.

Taking notes efficiently is, obviously, the first study habit to cultivate. In your four years of college, it is conceivable that you will be taking up to 1,000 hours of notes. It makes sense, then, to develop and learn a shorthand system of writing that will make your study life easier.

I used a shorthand system based on one developed by William Allan Brooks that incorporates the letters of the alphabet and marks of punctuation to construct words, phrases, and sentences. Its structure was logical to me, and soon I was able to take notes significantly faster than my classmates – without rushing.

When you are taking notes, you are doing two things: writing certain phrases verbatim and paraphrasing what your instructor is saying. Using an alphabetic shorthand system will give you some time to think before actually writing your notes down. This gives you an advantage of deciding what you want to include, without feeling as if you are being rushed. When you take STEM courses (science, technology, engineering, math) and the biologic sciences, you will be able to record a lot of factual information clearly. The better your notes, the better you will be able to remember facts, principles, and theories. The essence of alphabetic shorthand is the use of easy abbreviations for commonly used words. In addition, capital letters and punctuation marks are used as affixes (prefixes and suffixes).

Start using a few abbreviations and affixes until you feel comfortable with the system. The ones in the system I use are not difficult to remember, although you can invent your own abbreviations if you prefer. Feel free to create your own abbreviations for frequently used words in a particular subject. For example, you can use "hx" for *history*, or "lng" for *language*.

As an aside, I'll tell you that I had an epiphany a month or so before my college graduation. It was as if a switch had been turned on. Suddenly, I was able to see a greater interrelatedness between seemingly disparate pieces of knowledge and information. I wasn't any smarter – I just saw things more comprehensively. This epiphany may have come primarily from my schooling, but I also believe it came from using alphabetic shorthand. In using alphabetic shorthand, you are creating quasi-symbols for words. A word in itself is a symbol, so in a way you are substituting more efficient symbols for inefficient ones. Since you are also using conventional words in your notes, you will have a combination of various symbols to translate when reviewing them. Taking notes this way forces you to think differently. My seven years of education after college in dental school, research, and graduate school were much easier after having mastered alphabetic shorthand.

There are additional note-taking strategies that can be very helpful. One is to rewrite your notes clearly and logically. Leave out all information you feel is irrelevant. Everyone I knew who rewrote their class notes got higher grades in their courses. A second method is to cross out unnecessary information, thereby saving a lot of time re-reading irrelevant material. Immediate review of notes will give you a clear edge in your studies. Rewriting your notes will give you a better edge. Using alphabetic shorthand – either my version or one of your own devising – will hone that edge to its ultimate sharpness.

Starting Your Own Shorthand System – Some Suggestions

There are quite a few words and symbols used in this system. Write the abbreviations you want to start using on a 3x5 or 5x8 card or on paper. Add more abbreviations as you become more proficient. Start with some everyday words, a few punctuation marks, and some capital letters. Later on, you can add lower case/ upper case combinations.

Some common words and their symbols are listed here:

the -	all l	my m.
that -t	from fr	most m--
then -n	if .f	has hs
this -s	to t	had hd
these -se	of v	can kn
them -m	at @	but bt
there –re	an a	have hv
they -y	and &	whereas wras
me m	are r	your ur
or o	you u	do d
he e	is z	be b
for f	in n	with w

When "the" or "th" starts a word, use a dash. For example, "—t" is *that*; "—s" is *this*; "—se" is *these*.

When "-est"," –ist', "-ast" ends a word, use a dash. For example, "m—" is *most*; "b—"is *best*.

Other abbreviations for frequently used words are below:

Left parenthesis (w or wh when beginning a word
Right parenthesis)   sh when beginning a word
    For example,)l is *shall*;)d is *should*;)e is *she*; (el is *well*; (s is *was*; (l is *will*; (n is *when*; (t is *what*; (tvr is *whatever*; (m is *whom*; (r is *where*; and so on.

Several commonly used suffixes are:
, –ing [example go, is *going*; com, is *coming*; be, is *being*]
! -sion or -tion [example transi! is *transition*; posi! is *position*; situa! is *situation*]
+ -ent, -ant, -end. –and [example w+ is *went*; s+ is *sent*; h+ is *hand*; independ+ or indep++ is *independent*]

Additional abbreviations are as follows:

cannot	knt	lie	li or l.
easy	ez	very	vr
go	g	think	-nk
could	kd	thing	-,
say	sa	some	sm
until	ntl	first	1—
new	nu	more	mo
time	tm	next	nx

Start with a few of these and add more as you become more comfortable with the system.

Capital (upper case) letters are used for many common affixes. Their meanings often are determined by the context of the material you are noting.

Prefixes:

C circum (Cstance is *circumstance*)
T trans (Tlate is *translate*; Tsient is *transient*)
D dis, des (Dorder is *disorder*; Dperate is *desperate*)
M mis (Msion is *mission*; Mtake is *mistake*)
K col, cog, com, con, cor (KMsion is *commission*; Kduct is *conduct*)
A accom, accor, accum (Aplish is *accomplish*; Adingly is *accordingly*)
P pr, per, pur, pro, pre (Pfix is *prefix*; Ptend is *pretend*; Pson is *person*)
R recor, recom, recog, recon (Rding is *recording*; Rmend is *recommend*; Rnize is *recognize*)
X extra (Xdite is *extradite*; Xtraneous is *extraneous*; Xordinary is *extraordinary*)
L liter (Lature is *literature*; Lal is *literal*)
I inter, intro (Iest is *interest*; Iduce is *introduce*)
U ulta, ulte, ulti (Umate is *ultimate*; Urior is *ulterior*)
N insta, inste, insti (Ntute is *institute*; N+ is *instant*)
H hydra, hydro (Hphobia is *hydrophobia*; Hte is *hydrate*)

Suffixes:

V ive, sive, tive (expanV is *expansive*; resV is *restive*; endV is *endive*)
J cient, science, tience (profiJ is *proficient*; conJ is *conscience*; paJ is *patience*)
D tude, tute (attiD is *attitude*; destiD is *destitute*)
G alogy, ology, ulogy (geG is *geology*; anthG is *anthology*)
R ure (censR is *censure*)
P ple (triP is *triple*; purP is *purple*)
B ble, able, ible, ably, ibly (likB is *likeable*; liaB is *liable*; legB is *legibly*)
T atic, etic, itic, otic (exT is *exotic*; frenT is *frenetic*; ecstT is *ecstatic*)
F ful, fully (fanciF is *fanciful*; respectF is *respectfully*)

Other shortcuts:

vks *of course*
nsmcs *inasmuch as*
sls *as well as*
nsfrs *in so far as*
eg *for example*
ie *that is*
vnth *even though*
btls *but also*
m&m *more and more*
nspv *in spite of*
mrvr *moreover*
hwvr *however*
? *I don't understand this*

The abbreviations I use the most are:

- the common words listed at the beginning of this section
- (for w or wh when beginning a word; for example - (n is *when*; (i is *why*, (o is *who*, (r is *where*, (el is *well*, (t is *what*
-) for sh when beginning a word; for example —)l is *shall*,) d is *should*
- , for –ing
- ! for –sion or –tion
- + for –ent, -ant, -ent
- / for –ly
- prefixes P, C, T, A
- suffixes B, V, G

Use what you are comfortable with and start slowly. The time and effort it takes to master alphabetic shorthand is well worth it.

Taking Exams

There is only one approach to doing well on exams. Very simply, it is preparation. Assignments have to be completed and class notes fully understood.

Knowing my class notes and reviewing assignments gave me a total picture and enabled me to be prepared to answer any question. Start reviewing your notes and assignments at least a week before the exam. Talk to students who have already taken the course and ask them for suggestions. Focus on key areas with classmates and have a "study buddy" to help you with any difficulty in understanding. Fraternities and other groups may have past exams on file that can be used as study guides.

The format of exams can vary according to the instructors' preferences. Objective tests require memorizing many facts. Essay tests require writing skills that incorporate relevant factual information clearly. Understand the type of test you will be taking and study for it accordingly.

Leave the last night of studying for yourself alone, with no distractions from other people. Have a specific cut-off time for stopping that night. You may want to do a brief final review on the morning of the exam.

Try to get a good night's sleep before the exam, which is easier said than done. Everyone goes through "all nighters," but try to keep these to a minimum. I tried using "pep pills" a few times when I was in college. I was so wide awake I had trouble focusing on the study material. It turned out to be a losing proposition.

Here are some suggestions to help you on the day of the exam:

1. Take a shower and dress appropriately and comfortably.
2. Eat an unhurried breakfast or lunch, but leave enough time to arrive early for the exam.
3. Do not talk at great length to anyone beforehand. I found it too confusing when talking with other students about what they did or didn't know.
4. Keep hydrated and sip water while taking the exam. Studies have shown that proper hydration enhances performance..

Exams should not be traumatic. Do the best you can and do not worry about it afterwards. Always try to figure out, though, how you could have studied more effectively and efficiently.

You will be acquiring knowledge all your life. Exams provide feedback about your study skills. Look forward to learning, and you will improve your chances for success in the real world.

Selecting
A Profession or
A Livelihood

How do you know what you should do for the rest of your life? It is a difficult question to answer, but there are a few guidelines:

- Know your strengths, weaknesses, inclinations, and wants. Choose work that utilizes your strengths.
- Be ready to switch gears, since there may be more than five job changes in your life.

- Read material that informs you of possible areas of work. For example, <u>Wired </u>magazine gives you great ideas for STEM studies; www.mercola.com may give you some insight into health fields.
- If you truly know your passion, by all means pursue it.
- Be aware of financial costs and time commitments to reach professional status.
- Interview or shadow people in professions that interest you.
- Do not try to save the world! If you live a positive, constructive life, you will be making a positive, constructive contribution.
- It is unlikely that your work will be glamorous. If it turns out to be, count your blessings! What is probably more important than the career you ultimately choose is the mindset you bring to it. Do your work with a genuine sense of service and a desire to improve outcomes. You will be recognized and rewarded for your dedication to excellence.

Lifelong Learning

At its heart, learning is understanding. Knowledge and solid moral principles are its bedrock. The mere accumulation of facts does not constitute understanding. You do need facts, however, to bolster your understanding.

There are several areas to focus on with regard to lifelong learning. This focus should be in productive areas since some ideas are far better than others. Areas of lifelong learning include:

- Your work. Whatever you do, new ideas come along that will make your work more interesting and productive. Use 5-10% of your disposable income to attend courses, seminars, and professional meetings. Discuss ideas with co-workers and other professionals. Your work will be more enjoyable as you continue your improvement. You'll find it to be more fun, and you'll probably earn more money because your work will not be tedious and dull. You'll also sleep better. Heed the counsel of trusted friends, but always make your own final decisions.
- Love. The major outlet for love will be your family. Cherish your life partner and your children. You'll have more happiness at the end of your life knowing you cared for them. If you learn to love your neighbor as yourself, your life will be all the richer.

- Play. You need time to get away from work. Your play can be whatever you enjoy – a novel, the theater, a visit to a museum, an opera, social gatherings with friends, gardening, or anything you enjoy. Keep your work and politics out of your play, since most people won't be interested anyway. Express your opinions politely if asked, but don't dwell on them.
- Spirituality. You will recognize the need for individual responsibility within a moral framework. Honesty in your dealings with others always is always noticed by scrupulous people. There is sadness in the human condition all too often, but love, prayer, and faith will help during difficult times.
- Become informed. This may be one of the more difficult pursuits. Pick your news sources carefully. Read widely; choose wisely. Just don't become a news junkie – it can be unnerving. When you are informed, you will be in a better position to persuade people who may not have your insight.

Balancing all these things takes time and requires work, but it is a necessary lifelong pursuit. Your primary pursuit as a student should be study; play should be your reward for doing your work. If you cannot believe in a higher power, understand the need for ethical and moral living.

Graciousness

Of all the life skills that need to be developed, graciousness should be a leading contender. Human beings are a social group, and we are constantly interacting with each other. The ability to engage in constructive social interactions will help immeasurably in your personal and career successes.

Graciousness can be defined as being pleasantly kind, benevolent, and courteous. It is not being just friendly, but extending yourself in small ways that show you care. Not arguing, smiling, listening, and being polite create an attractive persona.

Graciousness is not ostentatious or in your face. It is being respectful of other people's sensibilities. It has taken me decades to stop being mildly confrontational with people when my beliefs clashed with theirs. I wasted a lot of energy. Part of being gracious is being able to completely disagree with someone without arguing or being confrontational. Of course, graciousness does not mean you can't take a vigorous and principled position to defend your beliefs.

Part of graciousness is learning to listen. People are rarely heard. Everyone has problems and successes – listen carefully and draw people out when appropriate.

I am attracted to people for many reasons: their competency, ethics, kindness, and sense of humor, to name a few.

In general, avoid discussing politics, religion, value systems, and the like. While it's entertaining to have these conversations with like-minded people; you'll save a lot of time by not arguing with those who have a different world view of how things should be. It makes sense to learn how to be gracious. Observe people and why you are drawn to them, and learn from their example. Becoming gracious can be a lifelong pursuit. Give it a try! It will be beneficial in the long run, and you will enjoy social interactions and life in general much more.

Principles of Success

Obviously, you want to be successful. That is why you are reading this book. Although I am not a success coach, I can unequivocally tell you that there are many good coaches out there. One brilliant example is Jack Canfield, who co-wrote The Success Principles with Janet Switzer. The message is masterful and coherent, and the strategies work. This book should be required reading for anyone who wants a head start in his or her life and career. Another brilliant success coach, Brian Tracy, has written many books on the subject. Goals – one of his best — is a perfect starting point in your journey towards success.

Only you can decide if you want to be successful. Only you can make the day-to-day choices that will create a successful life for you. Of course, you need a clear vision of where you are going in order to effect a positive outcome. Just "showing up" isn't enough anymore. You need a clear foundation of success principles in order to make it in today's world. You have to make a clear contribution by offering a service, a product, or an idea that others value and are willing to pay you for.

Heroes

We all have heroes. They elevate, sustain, entertain, exhilarate, and educate us. They uplift humanity through their work and fundamental values. They exemplify service and excellence, sometimes quietly, sometimes in full display for all to see. They lead ethical and moral lives. They are transparent. Sometimes they are flawed, but usually less than most of us. My heroes have inspired me to contribute more. With regard to athletes, it is the hard work, discipline, competition, commitment, role modeling, leadership, and excitement that attracts me. I would want my heroes as neighbors and friends.

In no particular order, from many walks of life, both persons and entities, my many heroes include:

Jesus Christ; Mary, the mother of Jesus; Mother Teresa; Pope John Paul II; Mahatma Gandhi; Patanjali; Winston Churchill; Ronald Reagan; Margaret Thatcher; Dr. Martin Luther King, Jr.; George Washington and the Founding Fathers; Rush Limbaugh; Ann Coulter; Edgar Cayce; Sylvia Browne; Mark Steyn; Mark Levin; Juan Williams; Nelson Mandela; Erich von Daniken; Ruth Montgomery; Richard Young; Condoleezza Rice; Dwight Eisenhower; Zechariah Sitchin; George Patton; Kevin Trudeau; Robert Bork; Ludwig von Mises; Dr. L.D. Pankey; Thomas Sowell; Jackie Robinson; John Wooden; Roger Staubach; Paul Harris; John Silber; Michelle Rhee; Clarence Thomas; Antonin Scalia; William Faloon; Suzanne

Somers; Don Shula; Bill Bellichick; Lou Holtz; Dr. Sherry Rogers; Dr. Timothy Smith; Beatrice Trum Hunter; the Constitution of the United States; the Washington Times; National Review; Forbes; Fox News; Rotary International; Hillsdale College and Imprimus; the Bible; the Heritage Foundation; the Cato Institute; the Carlisle Indians; the 2001 New England Patriots; the 2004 Boston Red Sox; and the members of the military, past and present, who put their lives on the line to protect and defend us. You get the picture.

Compile your own list of heroes. My heroes are basically ethical, competent, kind, and entertaining. And they are tough.

Investing

Follow the advice of true experts. While there are many fine investment advisers, the one I would recommend you read is Richard Young. His Intelligence Report (www.intelligencereport. com), one of his many services, is one of the best newsletters around. Had I followed his conservative investing advice, I would have avoided many losses and saved an enormous amount of time and money. And I would not have worried as much.

I would suggest reading Richard Young's Intelligence Report for at least a year to learn his philosophy of investing. It is straightforward Graham and Dodd. Young invests for value, compound interest, and the long term. He informs you of his own investments. He has clearly established himself as one of the most astute investment advisers of our time. Focus on excelling at your work and let a true master do the heavy lifting with your investments.

Gratitude

Live your life with a sense of gratitude for your opportunity to be enrolled in college and for the intellectual gifts you have been given. Thank your parents often for the sacrifices they have made to educate you. Despite any obstacles that have arisen or are bound to arise, always be grateful that a commitment to your studies will put you in a position to make a difference in the world and help you earn a better living. Nobody owes you anything. Be thankful that you live in a country where you still can make choices in order to realize your vision and reach your goal of success.

ADD/ADHD

AHEAD was conceived and outlined more than seven years ago. The thought of writing it in large chunks of time was daunting to me, and I did very little to make it happen. I read at least 100 books and had random notes in different notebooks, as well as several thousand newspaper clippings, but I never knew how to retrieve them efficiently or make them work to support the thesis of my book.

My breakthrough came when I attended a presentation called "The Joy of Getting Things Done" at our local library. The presenter, Linda King, shared several straightforward, common-sense suggestions that really hit home. I realized that I was practically the "poster child" for ADD/ADHD and had been for practically my entire life. I had so many questions afterwards that I left her my phone number. She called me, we discussed my issues, and I decided to work with her as my coach.

I began with writing in twenty-minute blocks of time. These fit easily into the structure of my day. My coach suggested I set a timer and not look at it until it buzzed. When the timer went off; I was surprised — and pleased — that I was able to actually focus on one topic for twenty minutes. Using the program she helped me devise, I did more focused writing in three weeks than I had accomplished in seven years. This was not only gratifying; it made me confident that I could actually make a reality of this book that had been, up to this point, only a concept.

Although ADD/ADHD will always be an issue for me, I have learned that it certainly does not have to be a game-ender. While there are many productivity apps and books on time management (I know this: I have them all!), working with a coach was what saved the day for me, proving the old adage, "When the pupil is ready, the teacher appears." Every time I hit a wall, my coach helped me find a way around it. If you have any productivity, ADD, or ADHD issues, I recommend working with a coach, but make sure you find one who is trained and certified in ADD/ADHD issues. Like most life and ADHD coaches, my coach Linda works with me over the phone. After so many years of hesitation and frustration, it really was a joy for me to get done what I always wanted to do. You can learn more about her at her website, www.JoyofGTD,com or by emailing her at Linda@JoyofGTD.com.

Conclusion

Getting good grades and getting into professional or graduate schools will require your diligence and persistence. Take advantage of the recommendations in this book. How your life unfolds will depend on your morality, your work ethic, your continuing learning ethic, and application of the principles of success.

Be of good cheer, and go forward in peace. You are our hope for a better future.

Suggested Reading

Bork, Robert H. Slouching Towards Gomorrah: Modern Liberalism and American Decline. New York: HarperCollins Publishers, 1996.

Brooks, William Allan. A.B.C. Shorthand. New York: National Library Press, 1933.

Canfield, Jack. The Success Principles: How to Get From Where You Are to Where You Want to Be. New York: HarperCollins Publishers, 2005.

Cruise, Jorge. 8 Minutes in the Morning. New York: HarperCollins Publishers, Inc. 2001.

Forbes, Steve and Ames, Elizabeth. Freedom Manifesto: Why Free Markets are Moral and Big Government Isn't. New York: Crown Business, 2012.

Friedman, Milton and Rose. Free to Choose: A Personal Statement. New York: Harcourt Brace Jovanovich, 1980.

Funk, Dr. Wilfred and Lewis, Norman. 30 Days to a More Powerful Vocabulary. New York: Simon and Schuster, 1970.

Gilder, George. Wealth and Poverty. New York: Basic Books, Inc., Publishers, 1981.

Gilder, George. Wealth and Poverty: A New Edition for the Twenty-First Century. Washington, DC: Regnery Publishing, Inc., 2012.

Hannan, Daniel. The New Road to Serfdom: A Letter of Warning to America. New York: HarperCollins Publishers, Inc., 2010.

Hayek, R. Friedrich. Road to Serfdom. Chicago: University of Chicago Press, 1944.

Horner, Christopher C. Red Hot Lies: How Global Warming Alarmists Use Threats, Fraud, and Deception to Keep You Misinformed. Washington, DC: Regnery Publishing, Inc., 2008.

Lewis, Norman. Word Power Made Easy. New York: Simon and Schuster, 1978

Sowell, Thomas. Inside American Education: The Decline, The Deception, The Dogmas. New York: The Free Press, 1993.

Steyn, Mark. America Alone: The End of the World As We Know It. Washington, DC: Regnery Publishing, Inc., 2006.

Tracy, Brian. Goals! How to Get Everything You Want – Faster Than You Ever Thought Possible. San Francisco: Berrett-Koehler Publishers, Inc., 2003.

Von Mises, Ludwig. Human Action. New Haven: Yale University Press, The Ludwig von Mises Institute, 1949.

Yergin, Daniel and Stanislaw, Joseph. The Commanding Heights: The Battle for the World Economy. New York: Simon and Schuster, 1998.

About The Author

Dr. Ernest Marino is a retired periodontist. He completed high school in 1957 in Valley Stream, New York, and received his AB from Wesleyan University in Middletown, Connecticut. He attended the University of Pennsylvania School of Dental Medicine in Philadelphia, Pennsylvania, where he received his DMD. He was editor of the Penn Dental Journal while at the School of Dental Medicine, and then spent a year with the American Cancer Society performing diagnostic oral pathology. He earned a specialty certification in periodontics from the Henry M. Goldman School of Graduate Dentistry at Boston University. Early in his career, he taught periodontics part-time at the Harvard School of Dental Medicine. He was a trustee at Applewild School in Fitchburg, Massachusetts and maintained a private practice in periodontics in Nashua, New Hampshire. A Fellow of the International College of Dentists, Dr. Marino is also an active Rotarian. He developed some straightforward study habits that helped him immeasurably during his schooling and were the catalyst for this book. Dr. Marino currently lives in New Hampshire with his wife and their two feline companions.

Made in the USA
San Bernardino, CA
29 September 2013